Birth

ACKNOWLEDGMENTS

If the Being Together books give young people the answers they need to lead richer and more meaningful lives, much credit goes to those individuals who helped the author in every stage of preparing these books. Many gave freely of their time, knowledge, and experience, but my special thanks go to Robert W. Soll, M.D., Ph.D., *University of Minnesota Medical School;* Reverend Paul M. Youngdahl, *Associate Pastor, Mount Olivet Lutheran Church;* Reverend Thomas P. Hunstiger, *Pastor, St. Stephen's Catholic Church;* Adora Miller, R.N., *In-service Instructor, Fairview Hospital, Minneapolis, Minnesota;* Catherine Myers, R.N., *Head Nurse of Obstetrics, Gynecology and Family Planning, Outpatient Department, St. Paul-Ramsey Hospital and Medical Center, St. Paul, Minnesota;* James R. Bergquist, M.D., *Clinical Assistant Professor, Obstetrics and Gynecology, University of Minnesota Medical School;* Simon Davidson, *Family Counselor, Jewish Family and Children's Service, Minneapolis, Minnesota;* James Merrill, *Director of Child Welfare Division, Lutheran Social Service, Minneapolis, Minnesota;* and Barbara S. Teeter, Ph.D., *Lake Minnetonka Mental Health Center, Wayzata, Minnesota.*

JEAN CORYLLEL LIPKE

a being together book

Birth

Jean Coryllel Lipke

Illustrated by Robert Fontaine

Published by
Lerner Publications Company
Minneapolis, Minnesota

The Library of Congress cataloged the original printing of this title as follows:

Lipke, Jean Coryllel.
Birth. Illustrated by Robert Fontaine. Minneapolis, Lerner Publications Co. [1971]

55 p. col. illus. 23 cm. (A Being Together Book)

SUMMARY: Describes the birth process and the care of the newborn baby.

1. Childbirth—Juvenile literature. [1. Childbirth] I. Fontaine, Robert, illus. II. Title.

RG652.L56 1971 618.4 71-104891
ISBN 0-8225-0596-7 MARC
AC

International Standard Book Number: 0-8225-0596-7
Library of Congress Catalog Card Number: 71-104891

Second Printing 1973

A baby grows inside his mother's body for nine months. He starts out as a single microscopic cell and gradually develops into a human being. Finally he is ready to be born. He has developed a protective layer of fat, so he no longer needs the shelter of his mother's body. His breathing and digestive systems are ready to operate on their own, so he won't need his mother to eat and digest and breathe for him any more. His cozy, shock-proof compartment has become very cramped; it's time for him to leave it. The mother's body automatically begins the process called labor, which will send him out into the world.

This book will describe what happens in a normal *delivery*, or birth, and will explain some deliveries which are not so common. It will tell about breast feeding and about some of the things which happen to a newborn baby and to the new mother.

No one can predict exactly when a baby will be born. The average number of days from *conception* (beginning) to birth is 266. However, some babies get ready sooner, while others take longer than average. A doctor can give the mother an approximate "due date" or birthday by counting from the time she had her last *menstrual period*. When a woman menstruates, her body discards the special lining of blood vessels which develops each month within the *uterus* (**yew**·ter·us) or womb. This lining provides a place where a fertilized egg cell can grow into a baby. If the lining is not needed, it pulls away from the uterine wall and flows out of the body. However, if a fertilized egg cell is present, the uterus keeps the lining to nourish and protect the growing baby, and the monthly menstrual period does not occur. Thus the time of the woman's last menstrual period can be used to estimate approximately when the baby will be born. About four weeks before this due date the doctor will start checking the mother very carefully every week, in case the baby should be ready earlier.

There are some definite clues to the baby's approaching birth. When *lightening* occurs, the mother knows the birthdate is near. Lightening means that the baby drops very low in the mother's pelvis. Sometimes this happens quite suddenly, usually not in a woman's first pregnancy, but more often with a second or third baby.

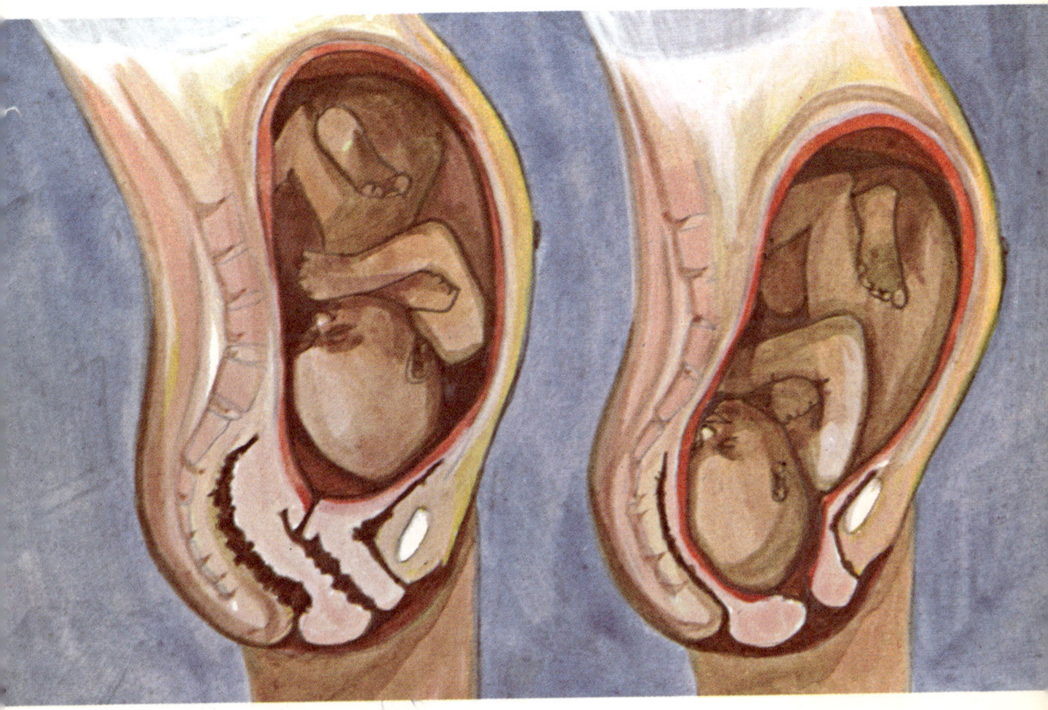

When the baby drops low in the mother's pelvis, she knows that the time for birth is near.

In a first pregnancy, lightening is more gradual, beginning perhaps a week or so in advance of the birthdate. The mother gradually becomes aware of pressure farther down in her abdomen. If she has been carrying the baby quite high, this change will be a relief. She will be able to expand her lungs fully again and take deeper breaths.

The reproductive system before pregnancy. *A*, uterus; *B*, cervix; *C*, vagina. The narrow opening in the cervix widens slightly during pregnancy. The process of labor stretches the opening so that the baby can move out of the uterus and into the vagina.

LABOR

Labor is an appropriate name for the actions which lead up to birth. The mother's muscles must work very hard, especially the muscles of the uterus. The uterus is the special place in the mother's abdomen where the baby grows. In the first phases of labor the muscles of the uterus exert a force of about 50 pounds per square inch to push the baby out. The baby must pass through the *cervix* (**ser**•viks), which is the name given to the narrow lower end or "neck" of the uterus. The tube-like cervix extends into the *vagina* (vuh•**jy**•nuh), or birth canal. Normally the opening in the cervix is very narrow, almost closed. By the end of pregnancy or beginning of labor, it may have widened to a diameter of one-half or three-fourths of an inch. The cervix must stretch to a diameter of about four inches to allow the baby's head and shoulders to pass through.

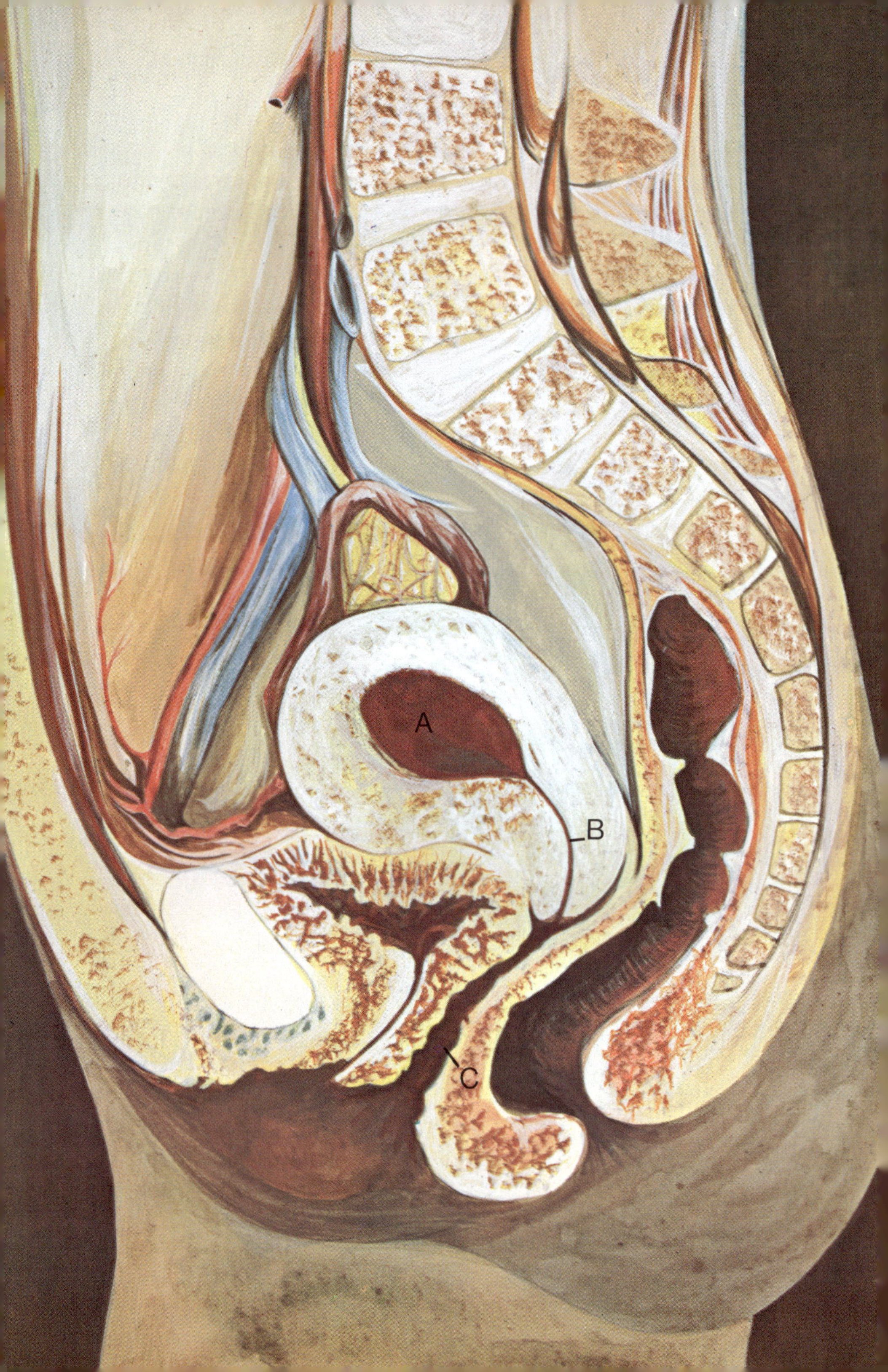
A
B
C

The muscles of the uterus stretch the cervix to the necessary width by growing tight and then relaxing. This is called a *contraction*. Actually the uterus has been contracting from time to time during the nine months of pregnancy as it gets ready for the baby's birth. The mother may or may not have felt these practice contractions. In some pregnancies they are so strong that if they occur near the due date the woman may mistake them for labor contractions. If the contractions do not get stronger or do not come at regular intervals, then she will know that they are "false labor" pains.

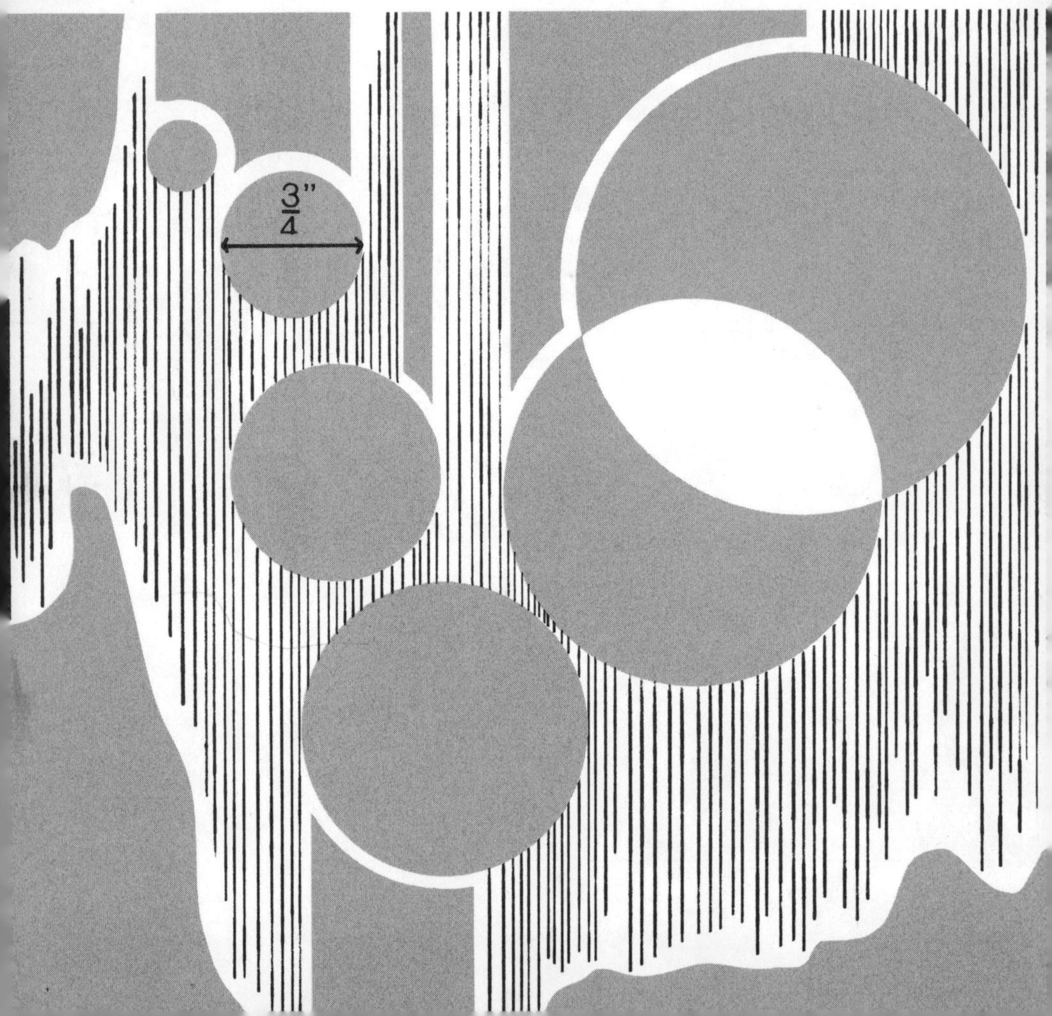

There are three stages to labor. The first is the opening of the cervix. The second stage sends the baby down the birth canal and out into the world. The third stage is the delivery of the *placenta* (plah•**sen**•tuh) or "afterbirth."

These circles illustrate the gradual widening, or dilation, of the cervix during the first stage of labor. By the end of pregnancy, the narrow cervix opening may have widened to a diameter of three-fourths of an inch. During labor, the contractions of the uterus stretch the cervix until the opening is about four inches in diameter.

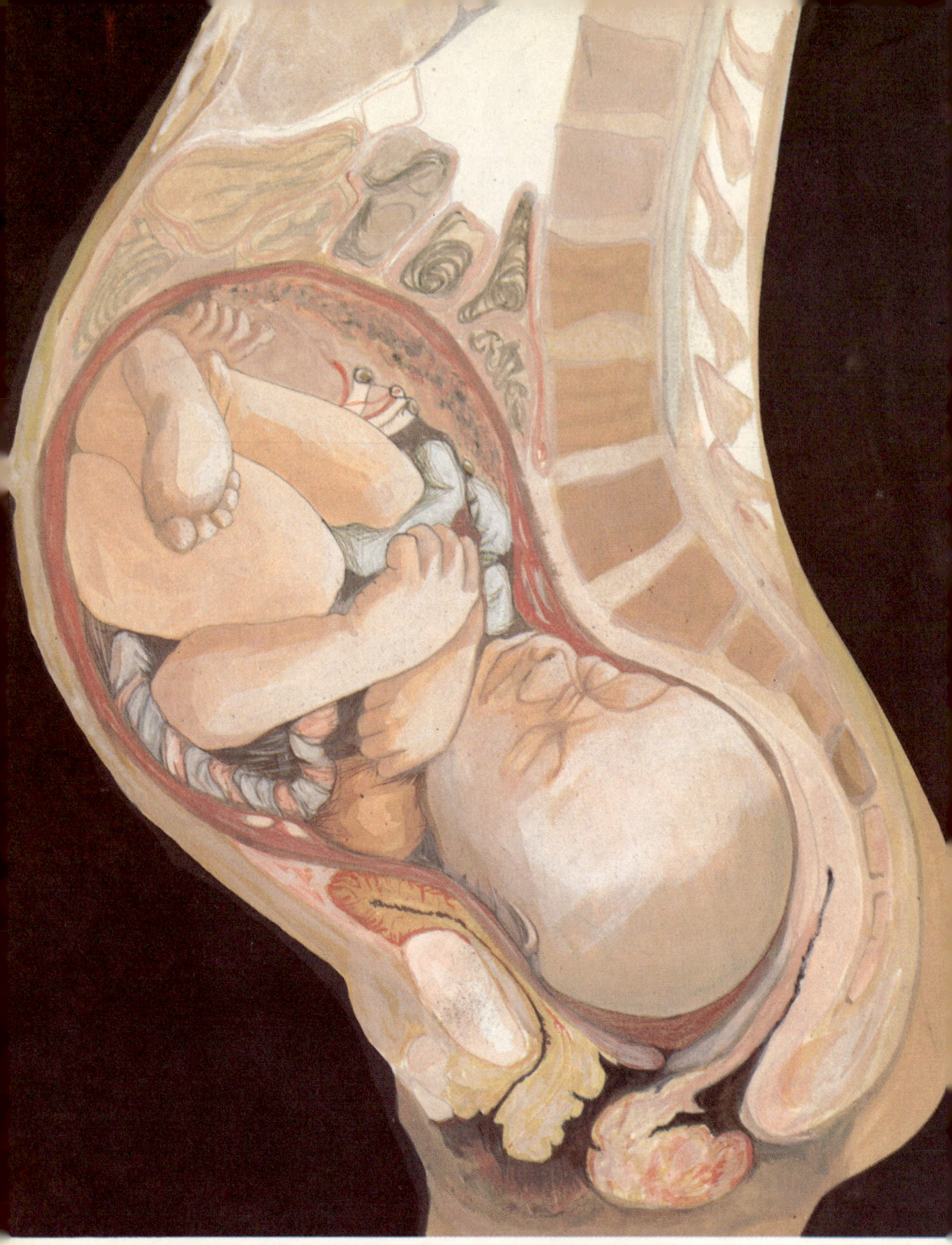

At the end of nine months the baby is fully developed and ready to be born. Labor is the process by which the mother's body expels the baby from the uterus and sends him out into the world.

STAGE I

Normally the uterus is about the size and shape of a pear and weighs about two ounces. In the ninth month of pregnancy it has grown to 500 times its original size and weighs about two pounds. In the first stage of labor the powerful muscles of the uterus, which have stretched and grown with the baby, begin to contract.

The uterus works something like a heavy elastic sock with an inflated balloon inside it. In order for the balloon to get out, the neck or opening of the sock must be stretched. As pressure is exerted on the top of the balloon, pushing it down toward the opening, the sides of the sock ride up and the neck opening has to stretch wider. It stretches until it is open wide enough for the balloon to fit through. Then the elastic sides and top of the sock gather together and push the balloon out of the opening.

So it is with the muscular walls of the uterus. The long muscles contract, pulling up the sides of the uterus and forcing the cervix to stretch. Once the opening in the cervix has become wide enough for the baby to pass through, the contracted muscles of the sides and top of the uterus gather together and push the baby out.

This first stage of labor usually takes from 3 to 16 hours. The contractions occur at regular intervals and thus can be recognized as real labor by the mother. They might start out lasting about 5 to 8 seconds and occurring every 15 to 20 minutes. Then, as labor progresses, the contractions will be closer together and last a little longer each time. When they are about 10 minutes apart they will last from 10 to 12 seconds; when 5 minutes apart, 20 seconds; 3 minutes apart, 60 to 70 seconds. These times are averages, of course, since every birth is a little different.

Besides contractions, there are two other signals which let the mother know that the baby will soon be born. The first of these is commonly called the "bloody show." During pregnancy a small amount of mucus and blood has been plugging the narrow cervix opening. As the cervix stretches in preparation for the baby's birth, this "plug" drops out. The other signal is the breaking of the *amniotic sac* (am•nee•**ah**•tic sak) or "bag of waters." The amniotic sac is the cushion of fluid which has surrounded and protected the baby in the uterus. It may break before labor begins, at any time during labor, or even just before the baby is born. The fluid may come out in a sudden rush or leak out slowly.

As soon as labor begins, a woman should contact her doctor. She should not eat anything; if she has a full stomach, her doctor's choice of *anesthetic* may be

limited. (An anesthetic is a substance which produces a loss of feeling.) The doctor will probably tell the woman to go to the hospital, so that she will have constant supervision and help. There isn't much a mother can do, for her body is working automatically on its own time schedule. If she relaxes, the muscles can work more easily, and the labor will probably not take so long. Sometimes a doctor will recommend medication or a mild anesthetic to help her relax. If she has had good care during pregnancy and knows what is happening, she will not be fearful and tense. Tense muscles do not work very effectively, so relaxation is important.

STAGE II

The second stage of labor usually takes from five minutes to two hours. Once the cervix is open, the baby usually moves down the birth canal quite rapidly. The powerful muscles of the uterus gather together above the baby and push. This is a different type of contraction and it produces what are sometimes called "pushing pains." The mother can tell when these contractions start, and she can use other abdominal muscles to help push the baby out. Sometimes the contractions will start before the cervix has stretched wide enough. The doctor may then ask the mother not to push until it has opened wider.

The vagina will stretch quite easily for the baby, but the vaginal (**va**•jin•al) opening may not. If the baby is quite large and the opening cannot stretch enough, the tissue will tear. Doctors often make a small incision (cut) to enlarge the vaginal opening. This is called an *episiotomy* (e•pee•zee•**ah**•toh•mee). An episiotomy prevents the opening from tearing and makes it easier for the baby's head to get through. The type of episiotomy used is determined by the mother's physical structure and the size and position of the baby. One type of incision is curved from the vaginal opening toward one leg. The other type of episiotomy is made straight from the vaginal opening toward the rectum. If the mother is given a local anesthetic, such as novacaine, she doesn't even feel the incision. It will be closed with a few stitches after the baby has been born. An episiotomy heals more quickly and with less scar tissue than a tear would.

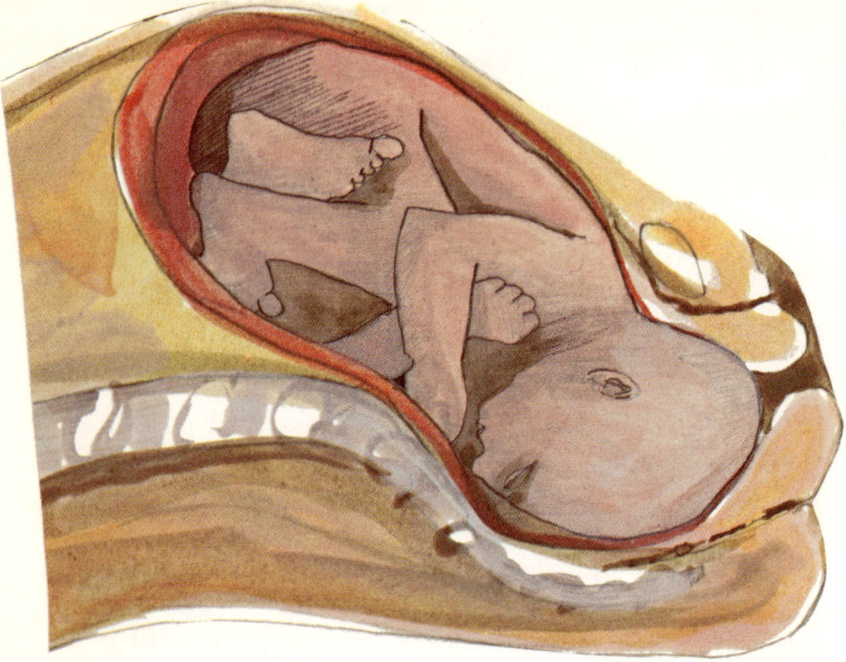

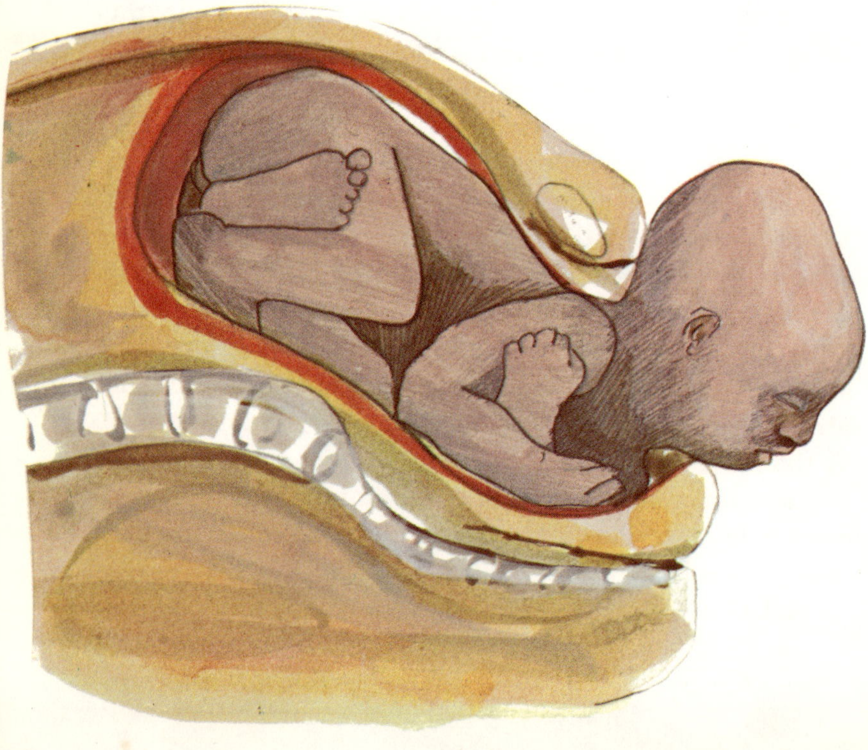

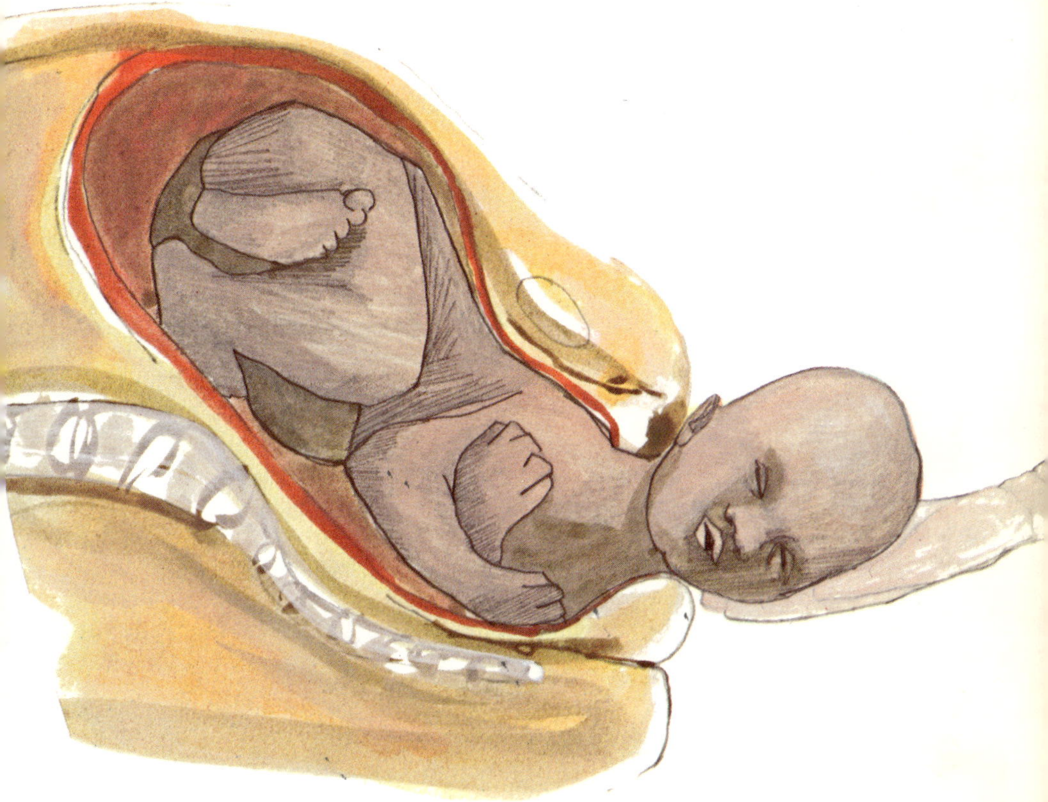

The baby is usually born head first. He is in the *fetal position* with arms crossed, and feet tucked up and crossed. His face is pointed toward his feet. If the mother needs help in the delivery, the doctor may have to reach in with *forceps* to lift the baby's head out. (Forceps are like large, hinged spoons.) Once his head is out, the doctor will gently rotate it to turn the baby on his side and bring one shoulder to the "up" position. While mother and baby rest, waiting for the next contraction, fluids and mucus are removed from the baby's nose and mouth.

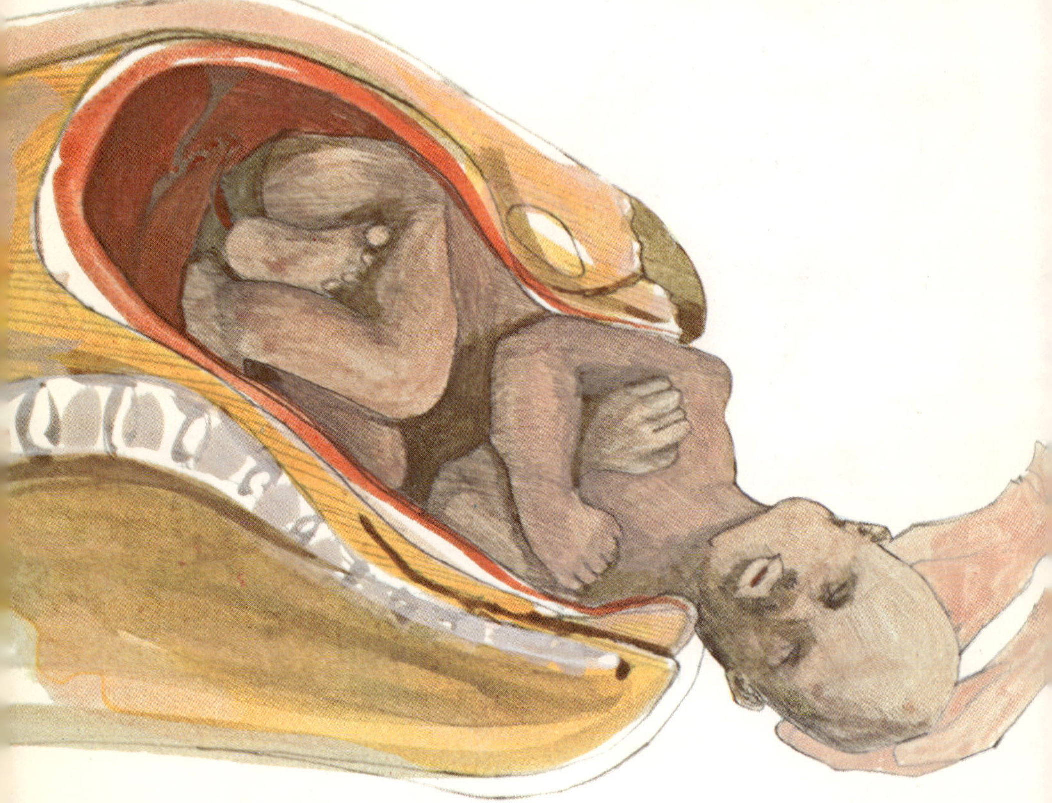

With the next contraction and push, one shoulder and arm are delivered. Then the other shoulder and arm are lifted out. Next, the chest is delivered and the baby can take his first breath by himself. The rest of the baby is delivered quickly. He is held upside down momentarily to drain out any mucus or amniotic fluid he may have in his nose and throat. If he hasn't started crying before, he will now.

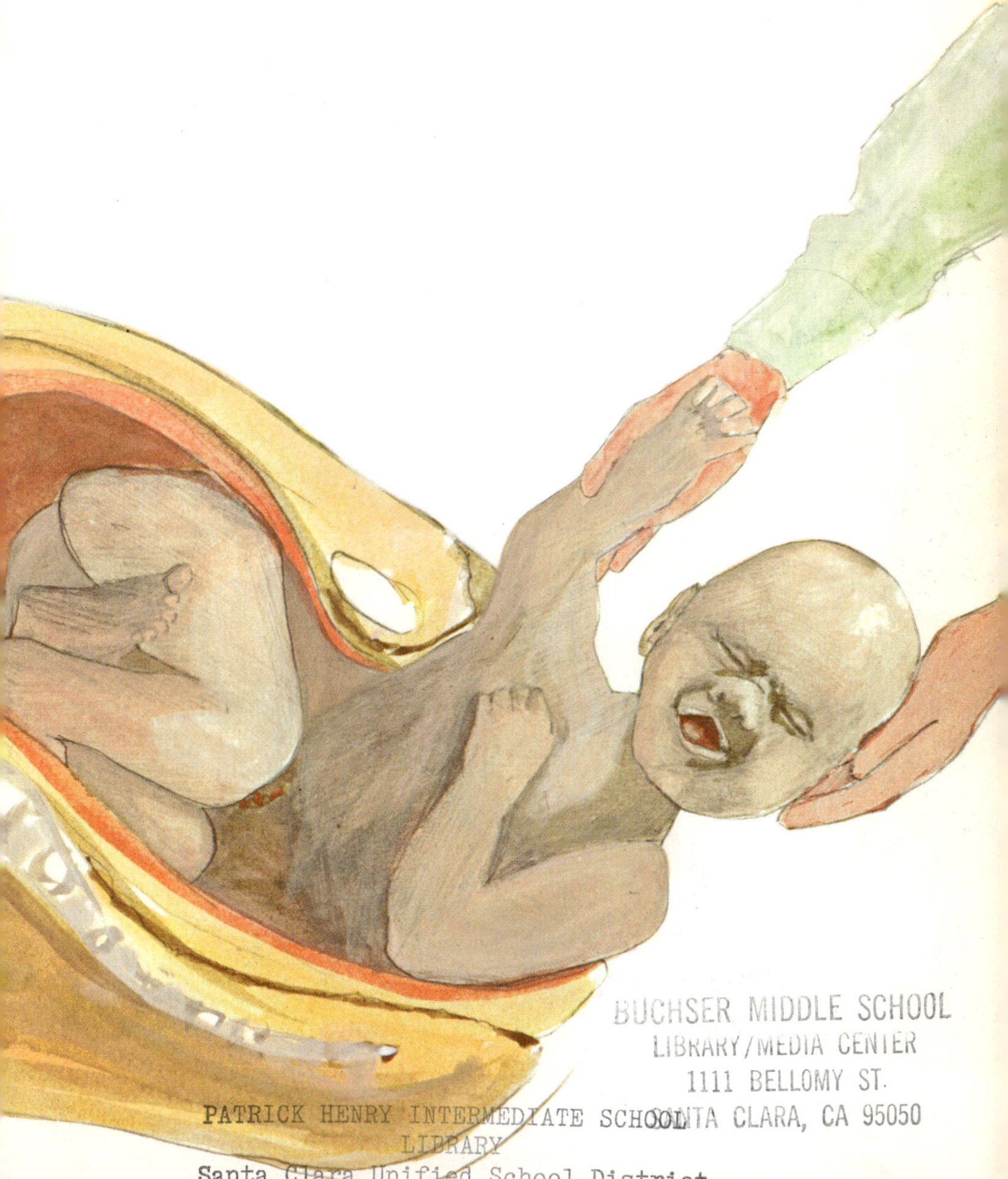

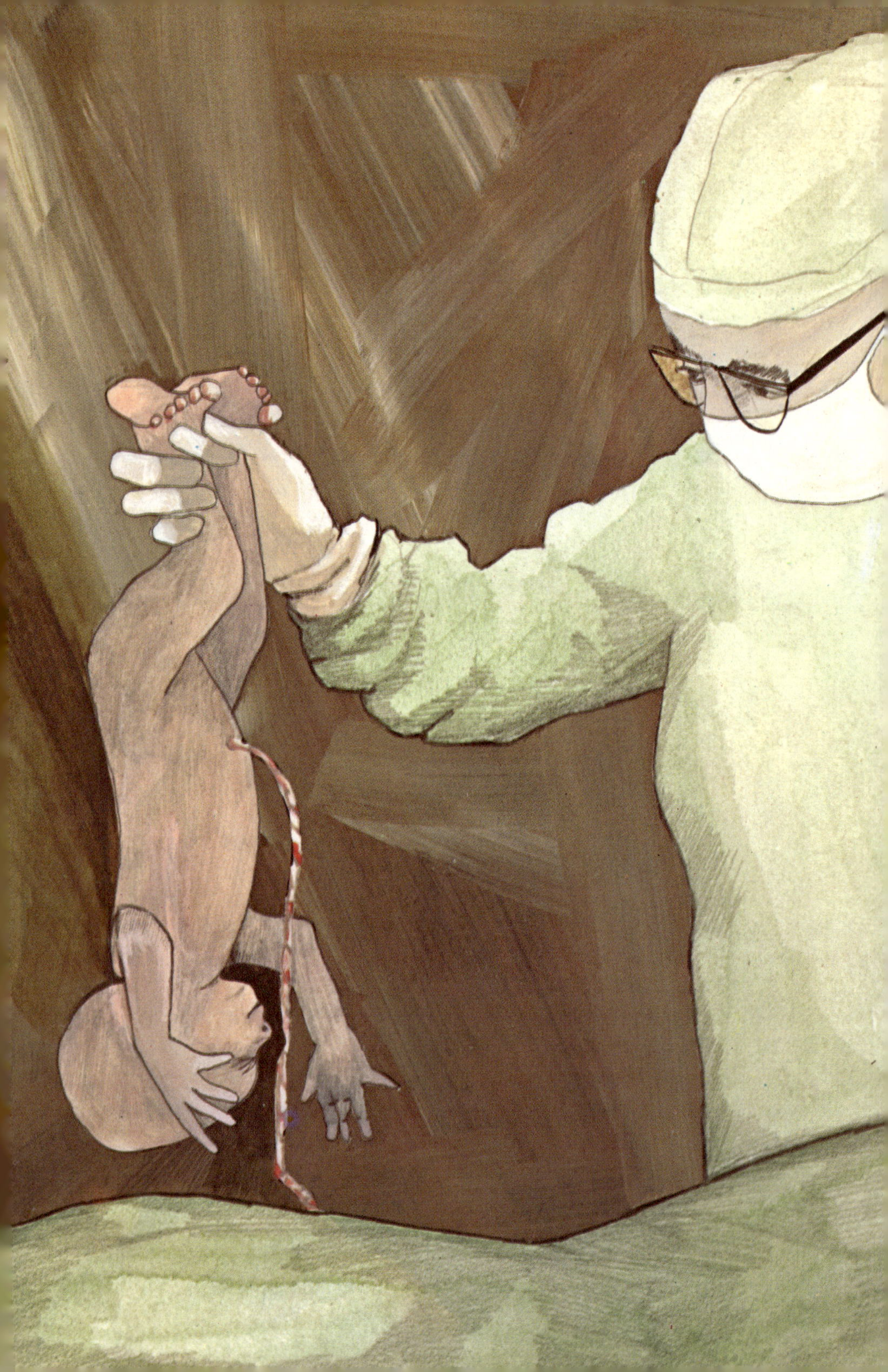

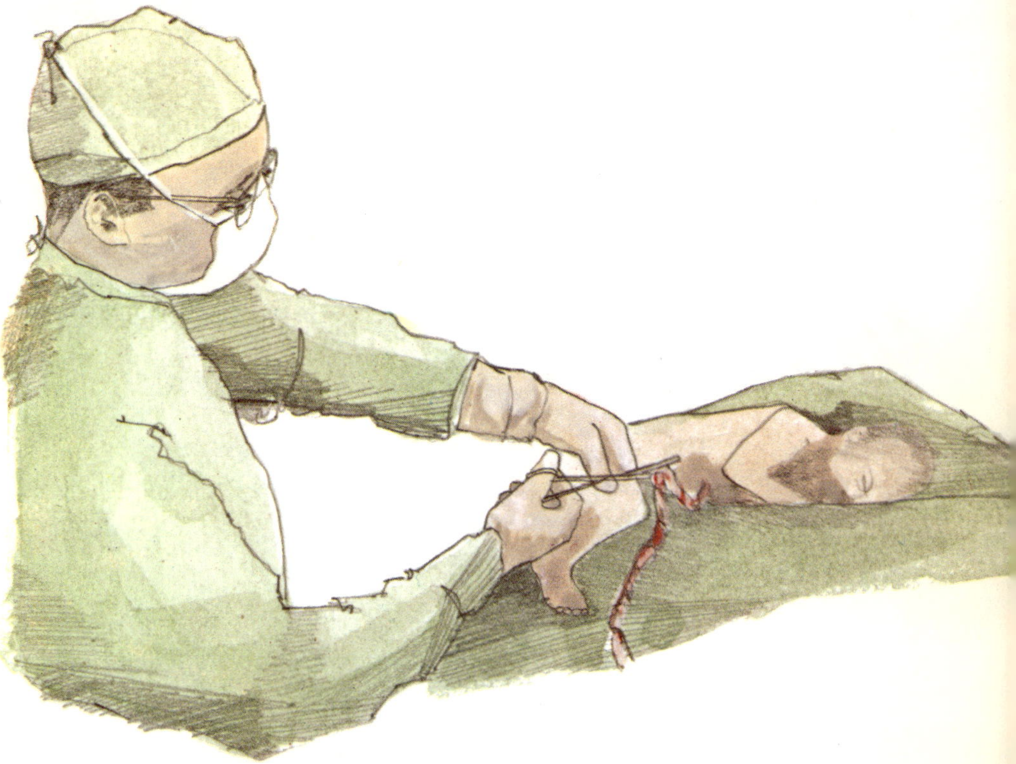

The next step in the delivery is clamping off the *umbilical* (uhm•**bil**•i•kal) *cord* and cutting it. The umbilical cord, about 20 inches in length, has connected mother and baby during pregnancy. Through it have passed nourishment and oxygen for the baby. The umbilical cord has also carried the baby's wastes back to the mother so that her body could get rid of them through her lungs and kidneys. There are no nerves in the cord, so neither mother nor baby feels the separation. Now the baby is completely on his own.

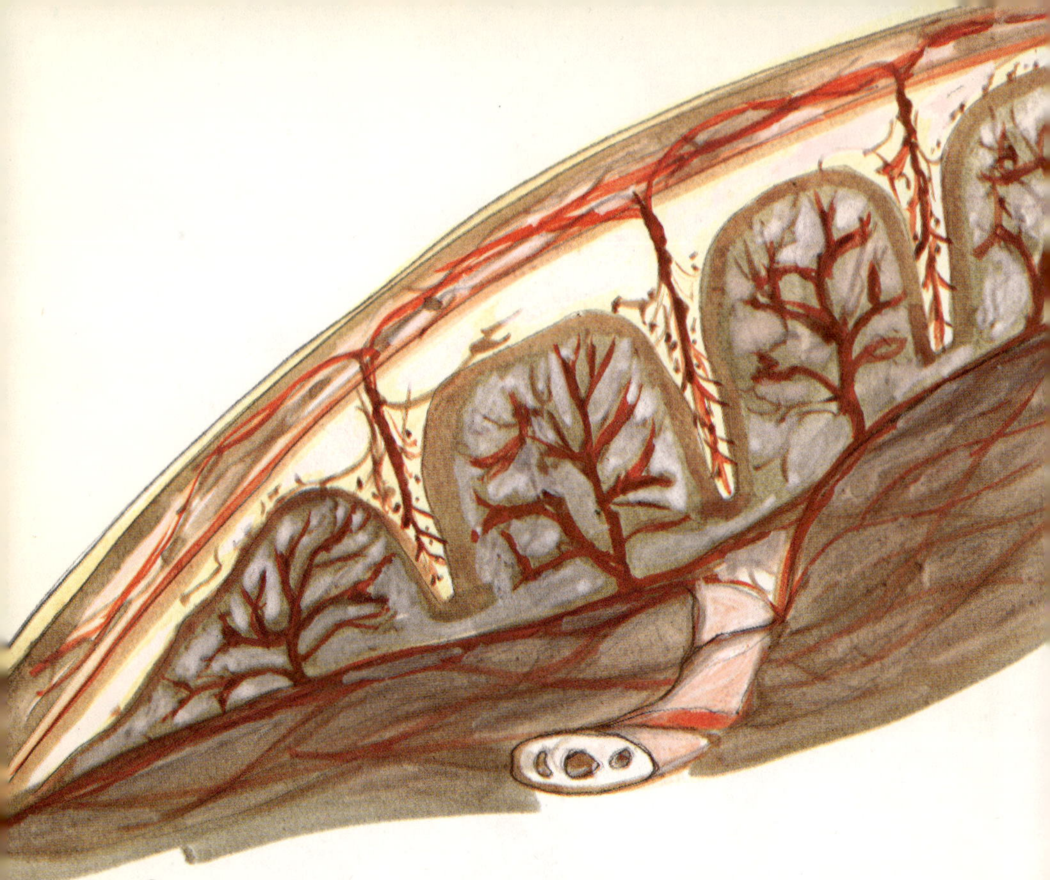

Cross-section of the placenta and umbilical cord. The placenta is expelled from the uterus soon after the baby's birth.

STAGE III

In the next 3 to 30 minutes the uterus will contract again until it has loosened the *placenta* or "afterbirth" and pushed it out. Usually this occurs within five minutes after the baby's birth. The placenta is the network of blood vessels inside the uterus which provided nourishment for the baby while he was growing. This unique, temporary organ is no longer needed, so the mother's body gets rid of it. A certain amount of blood and membrane will come out with it and continue to drain out in the next few weeks. Once the placenta is delivered, the doctor will stitch up the episiotomy, and the delivery is finished.

THE USE OF ANESTHETICS

The length and difficulty of labor and delivery are different for every baby. First babies usually take longer to be delivered. If the mother has had a good diet and good care during pregnancy, she will probably have a shorter labor than the woman who has not had these advantages. Relaxation exercises practiced during pregnancy and used during labor will also help to speed the process.

Some women demand a great deal of anesthetic and don't want to feel anything during labor and delivery. Other women are just the opposite. They won't take any anesthetic at all, so that they can be completely aware of the whole birth process. Most delivery rooms have mirrors positioned so that mothers can watch their babies being born if they want to. There are some anesthetics which can be injected into the spinal canal, so there is a loss of feeling only in the lower half of the body. This type of anesthetic must be handled by very experienced people and cannot be used in every delivery. Usually an anesthetic will not affect the baby unless he is very small. Then it must be used with caution.

Attitude has a great deal to do with the pain of childbirth. If a woman doesn't understand what is happening or what is going to happen, she may be frightened and tense. Tense muscles hurt when they work. Fear also causes imagination to exaggerate what actual pain there is. If a woman is strong and healthy and informed, her labor will usually be easier.

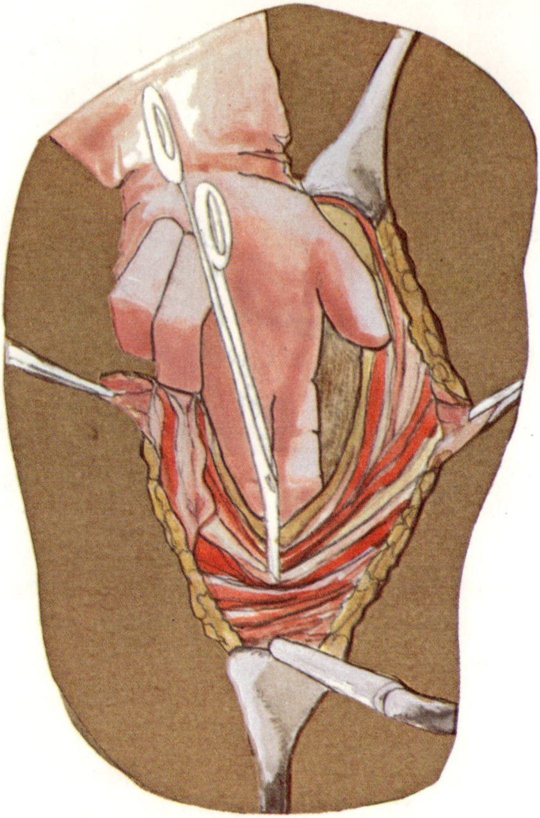

When a baby is delivered by Caesarian section, incisions are made in the mother's abdomen and uterus.

SOME UNUSUAL KINDS OF DELIVERIES

Some women cannot have a baby in the normal manner. Perhaps the woman's birth canal is too small to allow the baby to pass through. Or the walls of her uterus may not be strong enough to withstand the powerful contractions of labor because of poor health, an injury, or a previous pregnancy. Sometimes the baby gets himself into a crosswise position, which will make delivery difficult. For these and many other reasons, babies are taken from their mothers by *Caesarian* (se-

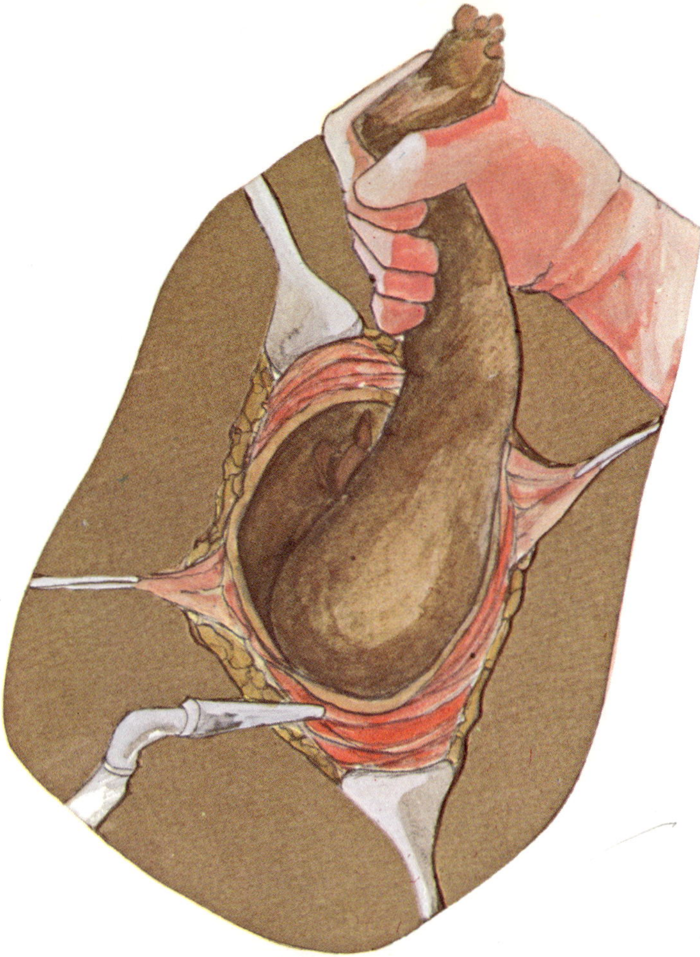

The doctor then lifts the baby out through the opening.

sair•ee•en) *section.* This is an operation in which the mother's abdominal and uterine walls are opened, and the baby is lifted out. It is called Caesarian because Julius Caesar was supposedly born in this way. If the doctor knows ahead of time that a woman will not be able to have a normal delivery, he will usually plan to deliver her baby by Caesarian section in advance of the due date. However, if necessary, a Caesarian can also be performed after labor has begun.

Some doctors will do a special Caesarian for fashion-conscious women. In order to keep the mother's abdomen scar-free for bikini wearing, the doctor will make a horizontal incision in the skin of the abdomen instead of the usual vertical incision.

Once a woman has had a baby by Caesarian section, she usually will have all her babies in the same way. This will depend on the reasons for the first Caesarian section and on the way in which the incision was made. It is possible that the scar from the incision in the uterine wall would not withstand labor contractions. The woman may have to limit the size of her family too, since each additional incision could weaken the uterus.

Mothers delivering by Caesarian section stay in the hospital a little longer, perhaps seven to ten days. The operation is major surgery, so it will take her longer to return to normal activities than it would take a mother who delivers in the usual way. A Caesarian delivery does not have any effect on the baby.

Another unusual kind of delivery is a *breech birth*, also called a breech presentation. It occurs when the baby comes down the birth canal feet first rather than in the normal head-downward position. Sometimes the doctor can turn the baby before he is born so his head will come first. A breech delivery is more difficult for the mother and harder on the baby, but in most cases neither of them will be harmed.

In some pregnancies the baby never gets into the head-downward fetal position but comes down the birth canal feet first instead. This kind of delivery is called a breech birth.

Sometimes a woman will begin labor and deliver before the usual nine months or full term of pregnancy are over. The baby will have all of his limbs and organs, but they will not be fully developed. He will not have the protective layer of fat acquired during the ninth month. His resistance to infection will be much lower than that of a full-term baby, and he may not be able to maintain his own body temperature. His chances of survival depend upon just how developed he is and how early he is born. If he is more than a month early or weighs less than five pounds, he is considered *premature*.

Premature babies must be given special care in an *incubator*. In this covered bed-container the temperature and humidity can be kept constant, just as it was in the mother's uterus. If the baby is having difficulty breathing, the incubator can also provide oxygen for him.

An incubator enables a premature baby to continue his development under conditions much like those that existed in the mother's uterus.

Malnutrition, illness, and accidents can cause an early delivery, but they do not explain all premature births. Twins are often born prematurely, but the babies are usually more developed than single-birth babies of the same weight and size. Once a premature baby has developed enough to maintain his own temperature and weighs over five pounds, he may be removed from the incubator. From then on he should grow and mature just as any other baby does.

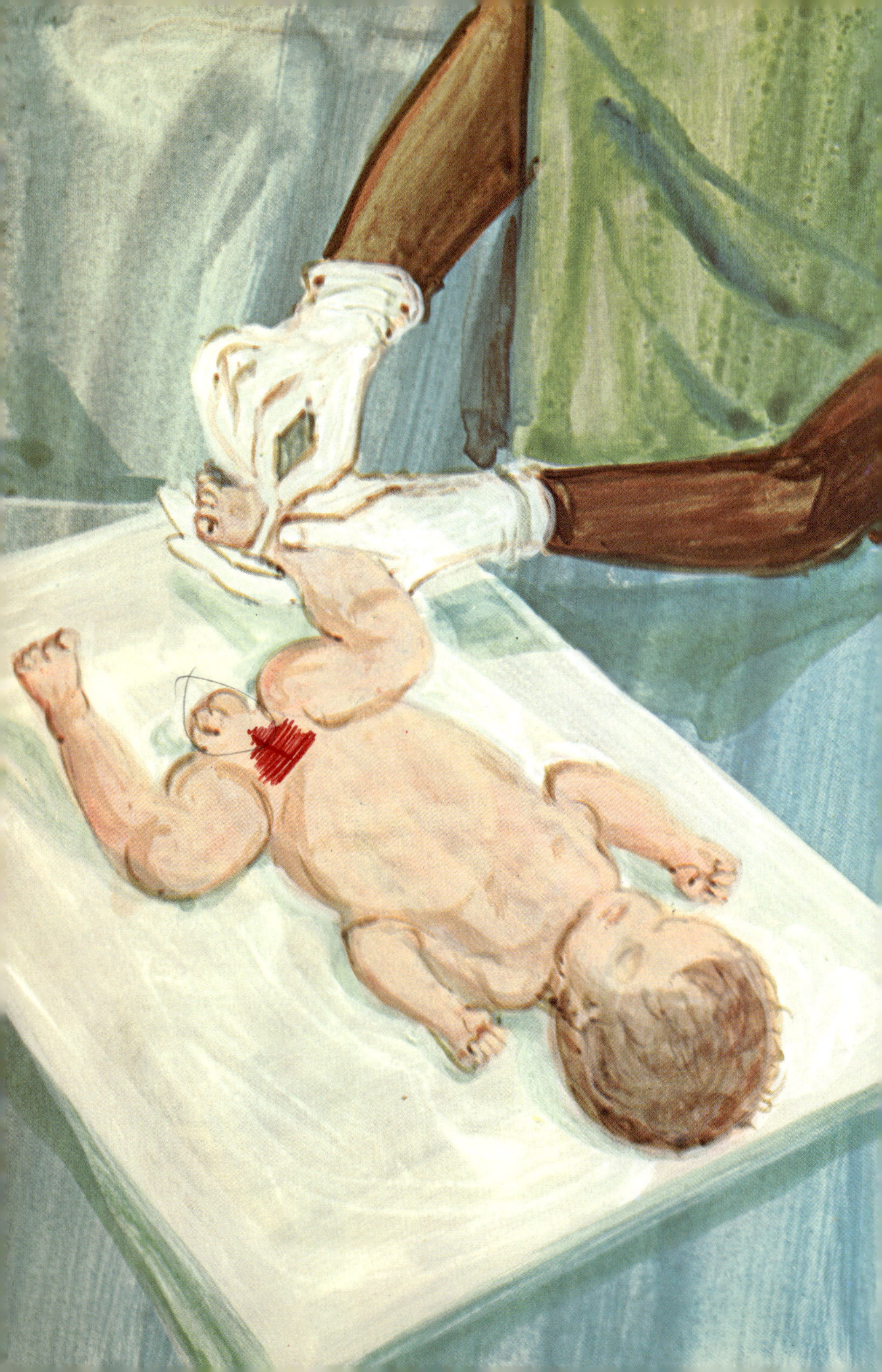

AFTER DELIVERY

Following delivery, the new mother will probably be exhausted and will want to sleep. The past hours have been exciting, but hard work. Before either mother or baby can leave the delivery room, matching identification bands must be put on both of them. These may be tapes or tags or beads or bracelets, but they are the baby's legal identification. Some hospitals permit a short visit with the new father at this time. (Most hospitals allow husbands to be with their wives in the "labor room," and some hospitals even permit them in the delivery room.) After leaving the delivery room both mother and baby are taken to separate "recovery rooms" and watched carefully for the next few hours. Some doctors consider this time so important that they call it a fourth stage of labor.

In the recovery room the mother is given food if she wants it. If she was in labor for many hours, she will be very hungry. Usually she will sleep. Every so often she will be awakened to have her temperature and blood pressure checked. The nurses will watch carefully for any abnormal reactions or excessive bleeding. The mother's abdomen will be massaged to help the uterus contract and return to its normal size.

During this period of recovery, the woman will sometimes have *afterpains*, which feel somewhat like menstrual cramps. Usually these pains are more severe after the birth of a second or third child than after a first delivery. Afterpains are caused by continued contractions of the uterine muscles. The uterus has gotten rid of the baby and the placenta and now it is "kneading" out the extra blood vessels and tissue that surrounded the baby. This discharge of blood and tissue is called *lochia* (**loh**•kee•uh). At first it is bright red in color, but gradually it turns brownish and then yellowish-white. The new mother wears menstrual pads to absorb the flow. It takes about three to four weeks for the uterus to rid itself of lochia. The afterpains caused by this process are usually noticeable only during the first few days following delivery. The mother probably won't mind these pains because they tell her that her figure is returning to normal.

After several hours of close supervision following delivery, the new mother is taken to her room in the hospital. She will probably stay for four or five days before going home. The new mother leaves the hospital about 20 pounds lighter than when she went in. Her baby usually weighs about seven pounds; the rest of the weight lost was in the placenta and amniotic fluid. Her uterus has shrunk to nearly normal size and her abdomen is much, much flatter. Some mothers will find that they have "stretch marks" across their abdomens caused by the stretching of the abdominal skin tissue during pregnancy. These marks vary from tiny white lines to scar-like tissue, depending on the elasticity of the woman's skin. Not much is known about preventing or eliminating stretch marks.

Emotionally a new mother may experience what is called "post-partum depression" or the "new baby blues." For a few days she may become upset easily or cry for no reason at all. A woman's emotional stability is greatly influenced by the balance of hormones in her system. As her body chemistry returns to the nonpregnant state, the hormone balance is disturbed. Until the period of readjustment is over, she is likely to experience some depression or irritability. In about six weeks most new mothers are back to normal, physically and emotionally.

The newborn baby must also go through a period of readjustment after delivery. The instant the umbilical cord was cut, he had to begin doing all sorts of things for himself. His body must take care of breathing, maintaining temperature, eating, and getting rid of its own wastes.

Either in the delivery room or in a special room for newborns, a thorough inspection is given the baby. A doctor checks his heart, lungs, sex organs, limbs, joints, and reflexes. The nurses wash off the creamy, white substance called *vernix* (**ver**•niks) which covers his body at birth. His eyes, nose, ears, and throat are carefully checked and cleaned of all amniotic fluid and mucus. Drops of a one percent solution of silver nitrate or penicillin are put into the baby's eyes to prevent infection. His height, weight, and sex are recorded. (In some hospitals other body measurements, such as the diameter of the chest and head, are recorded and a footprint, palmprint, or fingerprints are also taken.) For the first hours of the baby's life his breathing, heartbeat, and temperature are carefully watched. Some hospitals keep newborns in a special nursery until they are at least 24 hours old.

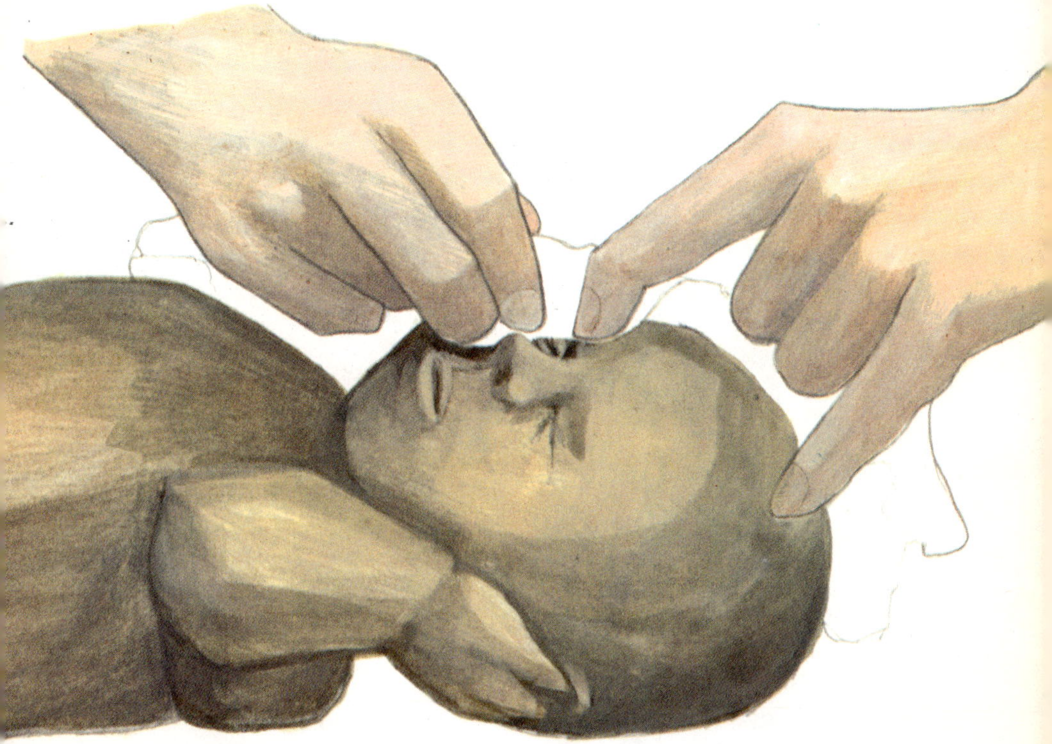

After birth the baby's eyes are cleaned and checked. Drops are put into them to prevent infection.

Before the baby leaves the hospital, many states require that he have a test for PKU. PKU is short for a rare disease named phenylketonuria. If it is untreated, this disease can cause damage to a baby's brain. The test is accomplished by simply taking a blood sample and checking it. A similar check is usually made again when the baby is six weeks old.

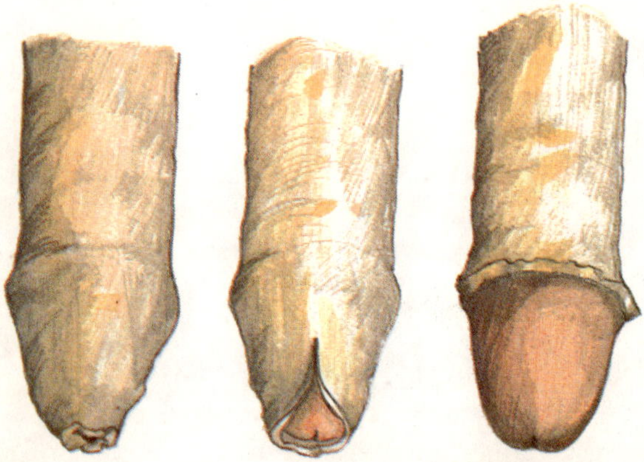

Enlarged drawing of a male baby's penis before and after circumcision. At birth the end of the penis is covered with a collar of skin called the foreskin (left). When a baby is circumcised, the doctor cuts the skin and removes it.

Boy babies often have a simple operation called *circumcision* before they leave the hospital. Sometimes it is performed immediately, while the baby is still in the delivery room. The doctor removes the baby's foreskin, the collar of skin which covers the end of the penis. Circumcision makes urination and cleanliness easier. If the baby is not circumcised, the foreskin may collect urine and a thick fluid called *smegma*, which can cause odor and irritation. In some faiths, circumcision is also done for religious reasons.

THE NEWBORN

The average baby weighs around seven pounds and is 20 inches long at birth. He will lose weight in his first few days of life. The weight lost is mainly water and is quickly regained in a couple of weeks. The larger the baby the more he will lose; sometimes up to 10 percent of the birth weight is lost.

The newborn's coloring may be somewhat reddish and his skin wrinkled and fuzzy. The baby's skin will smooth out in a few days and turn dark or light, depending on his parents' coloring.

The baby's head may look a little misshapen; this is because he helped in his own birth. When he was born, his skull was not fully hardened or grown together.

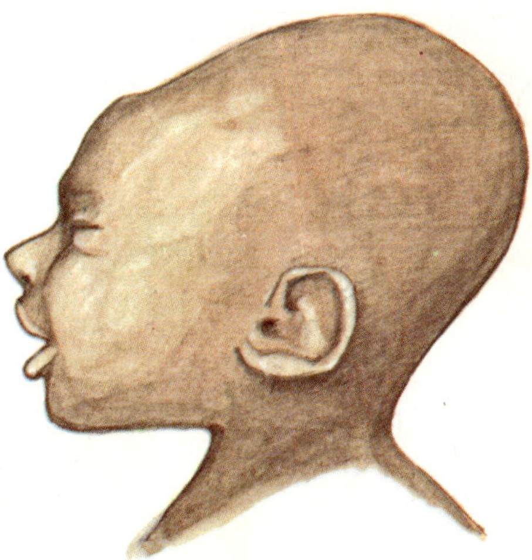

There were soft spots called *fontanels* (fon•to•**nelz**) between the bony parts; these spots will remain soft for the first year of his life. The fontanels, as well as the softness of the baby's bones, made it possible for his skull to squeeze together to fit through the birth canal. The shape of the baby's skull will return to normal in one or two days. His nose might be flattened for the same reason, but it too will shape up quickly.

The baby's head seems large in relation to the rest of his body. His chest is barrel-shaped and has about the same diameter as his head. In contrast, his stomach and hips are very tiny. His legs are slightly bowed because of their crossed position before birth. A one- or two-inch stump of the umbilical cord is attached to the baby's navel. It will dry up and drop off in about a week.

A baby cannot see very well at birth. He will flinch at a bright light, but he cannot focus on anything yet. He doesn't know how to smile or respond. His tear glands may not be working yet, so he may cry without tears.

There are many things which he can do, however. He can taste and hear and smell and feel. Four of the five senses are already well developed. He also has two very important skills: he knows how to suck, so he will be able to eat, and he knows how to cry, so he can call attention to his needs.

Some newborn babies can move around a little if they are laid on their stomachs. They will hold their heads up briefly and thrash their arms and legs. If unwrapped and held away from the body, the baby feels insecure. He will throw open his arms and try to clutch or encircle someone or something. Newborns like to be cuddled and wrapped tightly just as they were inside their mothers' bodies. They are used to close comfort and warmth.

A newborn will probably be very sleepy. He is tired after making his trip into the world. His body has had to make many adjustments and to begin taking care of all its own functions. He will probably sleep most of his first 24 hours.

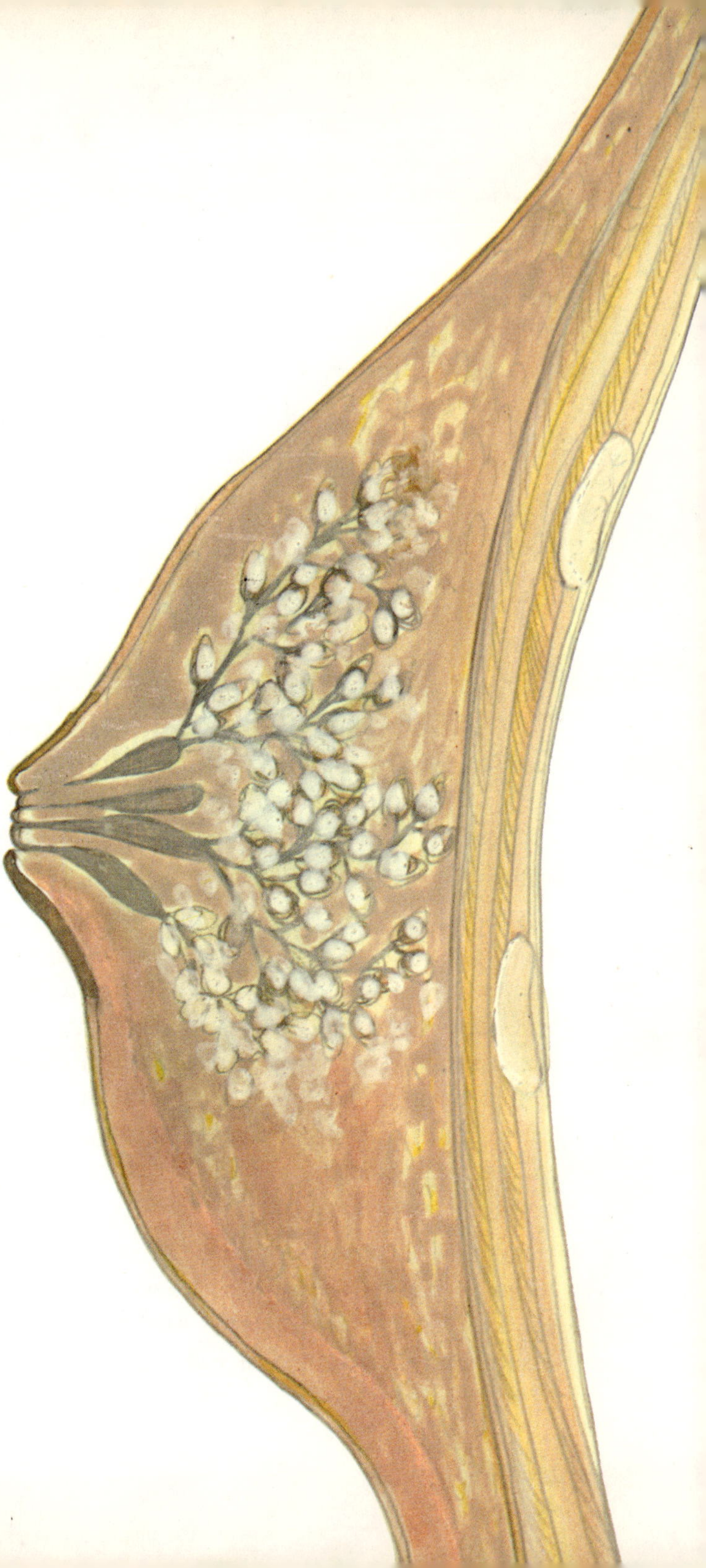

Breast milk is produced in small sacs called lobules, which are lined with milk-secreting cells. Numerous small ducts or tubes carry the milk from the lobules to the sinuses, cavities located near the front of the breast. From the sinuses several main ducts lead out to the nipple.

FEEDING THE NEW BABY

The baby's mother is also tired, and while she is sleeping, her body continues to work too. The baby will probably be hungry when he does wake up, and the most natural food for a newborn is his mother's breast milk. The first breast milk to appear after delivery is called *colostrum* (ko • **lah** • strum). It is a creamy, yellow liquid containing twice as much protein as mature breast milk. It is very rich in vitamins A and E and provides protection against certain infections. In two or three days, milk will gradually replace the colostrum. By the end of the baby's first week, his mother's body should be producing mature milk for him. Mothers' milk looks somewhat thin and bluish compared to cows' milk. It is easier to digest than cows' milk because of the type of protein it contains.

The size of a mother's breasts has nothing to do with the amount or quality of the milk she produces. The whole process is automatic; as the baby grows and needs more milk, the mother's body manufactures more. Most women could continue to breast-feed (nurse) their babies for as long as the babies demand milk. In many countries, mothers' milk is the only milk a baby receives for his first few years of life. In the United States, however, where sterilization and sanitation are fairly easy, babies can be safely switched to cows' milk whenever the mother chooses.

Mothers' milk is called the baby's most natural food for several reasons. It has most of the food elements a baby needs for growth. It is always the right temperature for the infant and is readily available. The newborn knows how to suck and gets satisfaction from doing so. The close, warm contact with his mother's breast also provides comfort. The warmth of her body and her heartbeat are sensations that became familiar to him during his nine months in the uterus.

Even though a newborn has never nursed before, he will usually know how. Cradled in his mother's arms with his cheek against her breast, his mouth will automatically search for the nipple. When he finds it he will begin to suck. He cannot see very well, but he does respond to touch. His mother has only to touch his cheek, and he will turn toward whichever side she touches and open his mouth. Some babies will suck very hard right from the start, while others like to taste and rest and take their time. Individual personality is already showing.

Some mothers start their babies on formulas immediately instead of breast-feeding them. Many excellent formulas have been prepared to copy the quality of mothers' milk. They can provide the same nutrition, digestibility, and taste. Since bacteria grows very rapidly in milk, great care must be taken so that all mixtures, bottles, and nipples are sterile. Some babies are allergic to cows' milk—it makes them sick. However, they can drink formulas made from other products. There are several formulas developed from soy beans which also provide the same nutrition as mothers' milk.

A baby will nurse from a bottle just as automatically as he will from his mother's breast. A bottle-fed baby should be cuddled and held closely while nursing just as a breast-fed baby is. Some mothers get their babies trained to nurse from both breast and bottle while they are still very young. Then the mother can be away from her child for some time and still know that he is happily being fed by someone else. If a baby is only familiar with breast feeding and his mother is unable to feed him, even for a short time, it might be difficult for him to adjust and accept milk in any other way.

Some women do not want to breast-feed their babies. Breast feeding means that the mother must be with the baby almost constantly in order to feed him every three or four hours, day and night. (A newborn's stomach isn't big enough to hold more than a few hours' supply of milk at a time.) If a mother has to work and be away from home and baby, she would have to prepare formula for the several feedings she would miss. There would also be a buildup in her supply of breast milk, which might make her uncomfortable and perhaps even cause the milk to leak from her breasts between feedings. In such a case, the woman would be wiser to put her baby on a formula right from the start.

Women sometimes avoid breast feeding their babies because they think that it will ruin their figures or cause sagging breasts. Breast feeding itself will not cause any damage, but when the milk glands are full, the breasts do need extra support to prevent sagging. Special maternity brassieres keep the skin and tissue which support the breasts from stretching. They are worn day and night during the last months of pregnancy and usually for as long as the mother is nursing.

Some mothers cannot breast-feed their babies. If the baby sucks too vigorously and the mother's skin is tender, her nipples may become cracked and sore. If they bleed, of course the baby cannot continue to nurse. Certain illnesses or conditions that the mother has had might also make it unwise for her to try to breast-feed her baby.

Other women do not always have enough milk to satisfy their babies' demands. It is important that a nursing mother be relaxed. If a woman is anxious, tense, or nervous about anything, her body may not be able to produce enough milk. A mother who is very busy doing housework and caring for other children may often be too tense to satisfy her baby's needs. Birth control pills can also diminish a woman's supply of breast milk. Diet is another important factor. A nursing mother must eat a balanced, high protein diet and drink plenty of fluids; she should probably drink at least a quart of milk each day. An inadequate diet may make it difficult for her to breast-feed her baby.

If a mother does not wish to breast-feed her baby, she should tell her doctor before the baby arrives. Then, at the time of delivery or shortly thereafter, he can give her medication to dry up her milk glands. Once a mother has begun nursing and wishes to stop, she should gradually work the baby onto bottle feedings. As the baby demands less nourishment from her, her supply of milk will automatically decrease. Medications will also help.

Eating is the major concern of a newborn's life. It is his most satisfying physical and psychological experience in this strange new world. That is why it is so important that he be fed lovingly. Babies can sense love and of course they know when they are not loved. Just as attitude is important in labor and delivery, so it is in feeding the newborn. Breast feeding can be a distasteful chore or a satisfying experience, depending on the mother's feelings. If she resents being tied to the house and baby, then breast feeding will not be pleasant for either her or her child. On the other hand, if she enjoys the intimate contact and finds pleasure in giving her baby what no one else can give him, then breast feeding can be rewarding for both mother and baby. The decision to breast- or bottle-feed must be made carefully, taking into consideration both the mother's ability to nurse and her desire to do so.

CHILDBIRTH TODAY

History shows that childbirth once brought death to many women and babies. Today modern medicine and technical knowledge have made childbirth relatively safe for both mother and baby. As already mentioned, there are many possible problems and complications, but with a doctor's care they can often be avoided.

The woman who for any number of reasons must deliver by Caesarian section can be diagnosed long before labor begins. If the doctor learns in advance that she cannot have a normal delivery, both mother and baby can be saved. Special diets and medications have helped many women carry their babies to full term, when without such care they might have lost them. Improved anesthetics have relieved much of the tension and pain some women feel during labor and delivery. Episiotomies prevent tearing and reduce the possibility of hemorrhaging (excessive bleeding). Sterile surroundings and precautions have reduced greatly the risk of infection.

Babies too benefit from advanced medical knowledge and techniques. The premature baby has an incubator to help him breathe and maintain his body temperature until he can do these things for himself. The baby born with a *jaundiced* or yellow complexion can be given an immediate blood transfusion. Severe jaundice is often a sign of a blood disorder related to the inherited *Rh factor*.* Today the possibility of an Rh factor complication can be predicted and prepared for. A fresh supply of blood of the baby's type will be ready in the delivery room, if the baby should need it. If a severe Rh condition is diagnosed early in pregnancy, the fetus may even be given a transfusion before birth.

When venereal disease was uncontrolled, it was a serious threat to newborns. Mothers having the disease often passed it on to their babies.** As the baby came through the birth canal, he would pick up the infection. Usually it attacked his eyes, causing blindness. Today most states require newborns to have drops preventing infection placed in their eyes immediately after birth.

**See the Being Together book* Heredity *for an explanation of the Rh factor.*
***Another book in this series,* Sex Outside of Marriage, *discusses venereal disease in detail.*

Having a baby is a natural function, automatically controlled by a woman's body. There are many ways in which modern medical knowledge and equipment can help a woman to have a safe, comfortable pregnancy, labor, and delivery. For the sake of her own health and the health of her baby, a modern woman should take advantage of all the help available to her.

INDEX